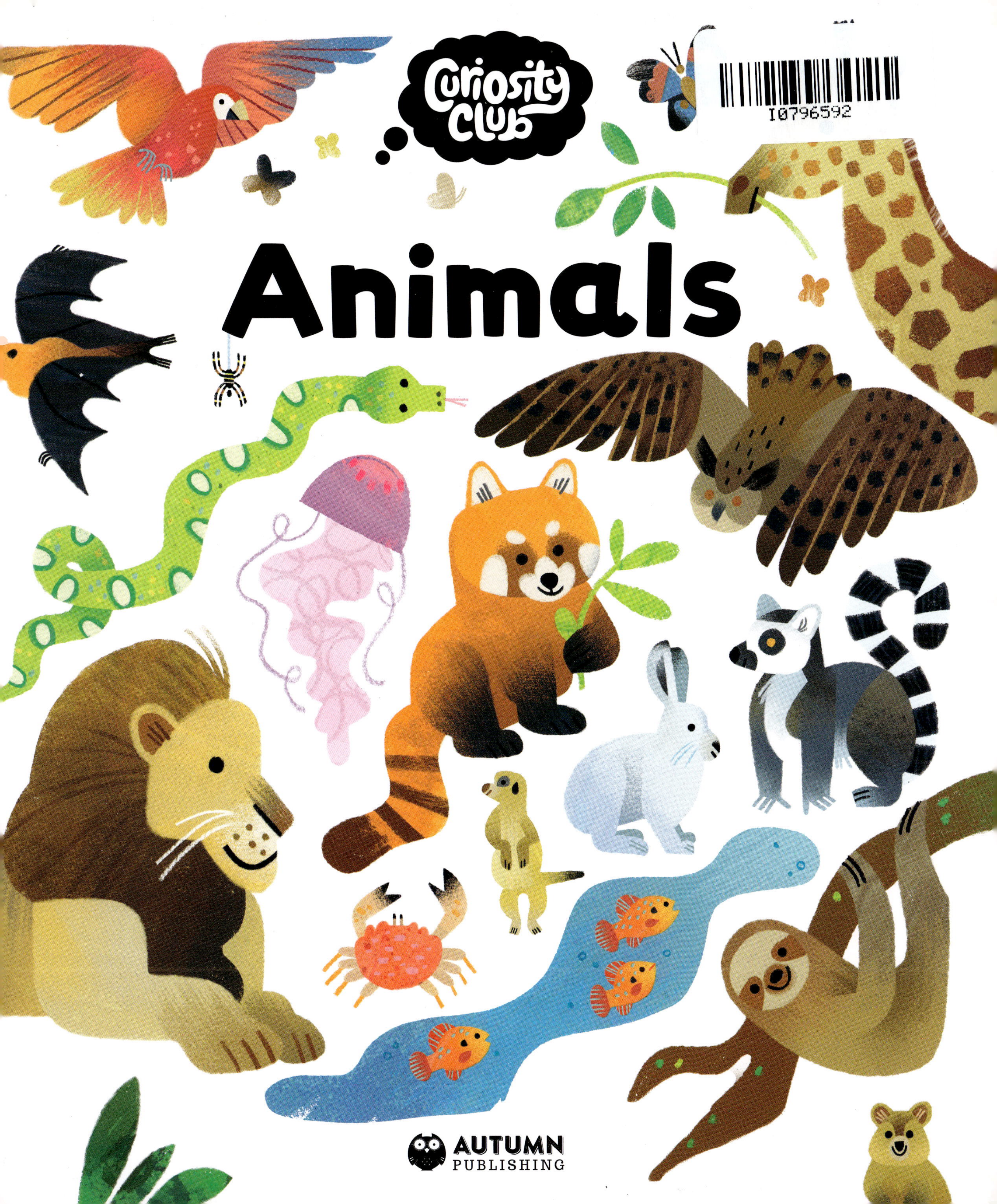
Curiosity Club
Animals
AUTUMN
PUBLISHING

Good to Know!

You'll come across some very useful words in this book! Here's what they all mean . . .

Apex Predator: an animal at the top of the food chain without any predators of its own.

Biome: a large ecosystem that relies on climate and terrain.

Climate: the weather and temperature of a place.

Ecosystem: when animals and plants all live together in one place and rely on each other to survive.

Endangered: when there aren't many of an animal left and there might not be any at all in the future.

Habitat: where a plant or animal lives.

Invertebrate: an animal with no backbone.

Predator: an animal that hunts other animals for food.

Prey: an animal that is hunted by other animals for food.

Species: a group of living things with the same characteristics.

Terrain: land or ground, and what's special about it (e.g., rocky or muddy).

Vertebrate: an animal with a backbone.

Contents

All About Animals!

MAMMALS
Mammals, like dogs, are vertebrates, and often quite hairy. Babies drink their mother's milk.

ARACHNIDS
Arachnids, like spiders, have eight legs. Unlike insects, they stay the same as they grow older, without a larvae stage.

BIRDS
Birds, like bald eagles, are animals with feathers. They have wings instead of arms, and lay eggs.

AMPHIBIANS
Amphibians, like poison dart frogs, can live both on land and in water.

INSECTS
Insects, like bees, are invertebrates whose bodies are made of sections (usually a head, thorax, and abdomen).

FISH
Fish, like angelfish, live underwater. They are vertebrates and have fins.

CNIDARIANS
Cnidarians, like jellyfish, are aquatic animals that have special stinging cells they use to defend themselves!

ECHINODERMS
Echinoderms, like starfish, are invertebrates that live on the ocean floor. They have spiny or bumpy skin.

MOLLUSCS
Molluscs, like octopuses, are invertebrates with soft, squishy bodies. They often have shells.

REPTILES
Reptiles, like giant tortoises, are cold-blooded vertebrates. They lay eggs and have scaly skin.

MARSUPIALS
Marsupials, like quokkas, are mammals, but females have pouches in which they carry their babies.

CRUSTACEANS
Crustaceans, like lobsters, live mostly underwater and have shells covering their bodies.

All About Biomes

(where animals live)

GRASSLAND
Grasslands, or savannas, are mostly flat and covered in grass and trees.

OCEAN
Oceans are huge bodies of saltwater.

WOODLAND
Woodlands are areas covered in lots of trees.

POLAR
The polar regions at the top and bottom of the planet are very cold, snowy, and icy.

DESERT
Deserts are very dry and have extreme temperatures.

RAINFOREST
Rainforests are wet, humid woodlands.

Northern Pine Forests

Pine forests are covered in trees. The shelter these trees provide, along with the mild weather, means the forests are home to a wide range of animals.

FOX
MAMMAL

Foxes are related to dogs and wolves. Their orange fur helps them blend into the trees and grass while hunting prey.

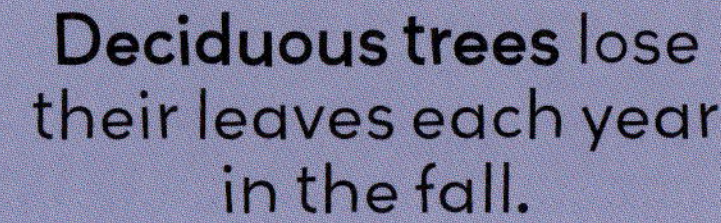

Deciduous trees lose their leaves each year in the fall.

RABBIT
MAMMAL

Rabbits are found all over the world due to traders, who brought them on ships. Their big ears help them listen out for predators like foxes.

GRIZZLY BEAR
MAMMAL

Grizzly bears are apex predators in the forest. Their razor-sharp claws are 4 in. long! Though they do love to feast on salmon, a grizzly's diet is also full of nuts, berries, and roots.

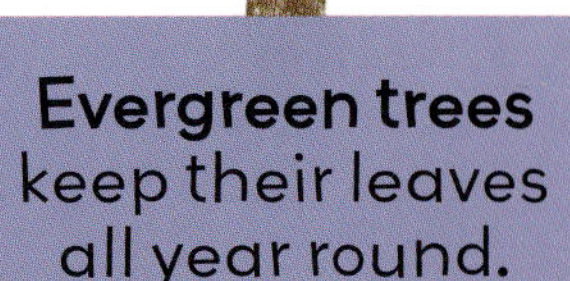

Evergreen trees keep their leaves all year round.

BARRED OWL
BIRD
Barred owls hunt at night, swooping through the forest like a pale ghost. They don't always look ghostly, though—if they eat too much crayfish, their feathers can turn pink.
FLYING SQUIRREL
MAMMAL
Flying squirrels have flaps of skin beneath their limbs to help them glide for up to 300 ft through the trees—that's almost the length of a soccer field.
MOOSE
MAMMAL
Moose are the largest members of the deer family. Their massive antlers mean moose measure up to 10 ft high!
TIMBER WOLF
MAMMAL
These wolves hunt and defend their territory in tight-knit packs. Their gray-brown fur helps them blend in. If they lose a pack member, they howl to find them again.

Bamboo Forests

PEACOCK
BIRD

Peacocks use their dazzling tail feathers to show off to females, known as **peahens.**

GIANT PANDA
MAMMAL

Giant pandas eat up to 84 lbs of bamboo a day. They need to have at least two different types nearby so they don't starve.

TIGER
MAMMAL

These big cats are famous for their black and orange stripes, which help them to blend into the background to sneak up on their prey. This pattern is unique to each tiger, like a human fingerprint.

DID YOU KNOW?
Bamboo is actually a kind of grass. Their tall, trunk-like stalks mix with ancient ginkgo trees to create wonderful habitats for all sorts of creatures.
RED PANDA MAMMAL
Red pandas aren't related to giant ones. Their name comes from the Nepalese "nigalya ponya," which means "bamboo eater." When scientists went to name the giant panda later on, they noticed the shared love of bamboo and named them "panda" too!
Over 1,400 species of bamboo live in Asian bamboo forests! The bamboo can grow up to 112 ft tall, with some types growing even taller.
When threatened, red pandas make themselves as tall as they can.

The Sonoran Desert

This dry, rocky desert stretches across Southern USA and Northern Mexico, covering an area 3.5 times the size of Ireland. The creatures living there have evolved to withstand scorching temperatures of up to 120 °F.

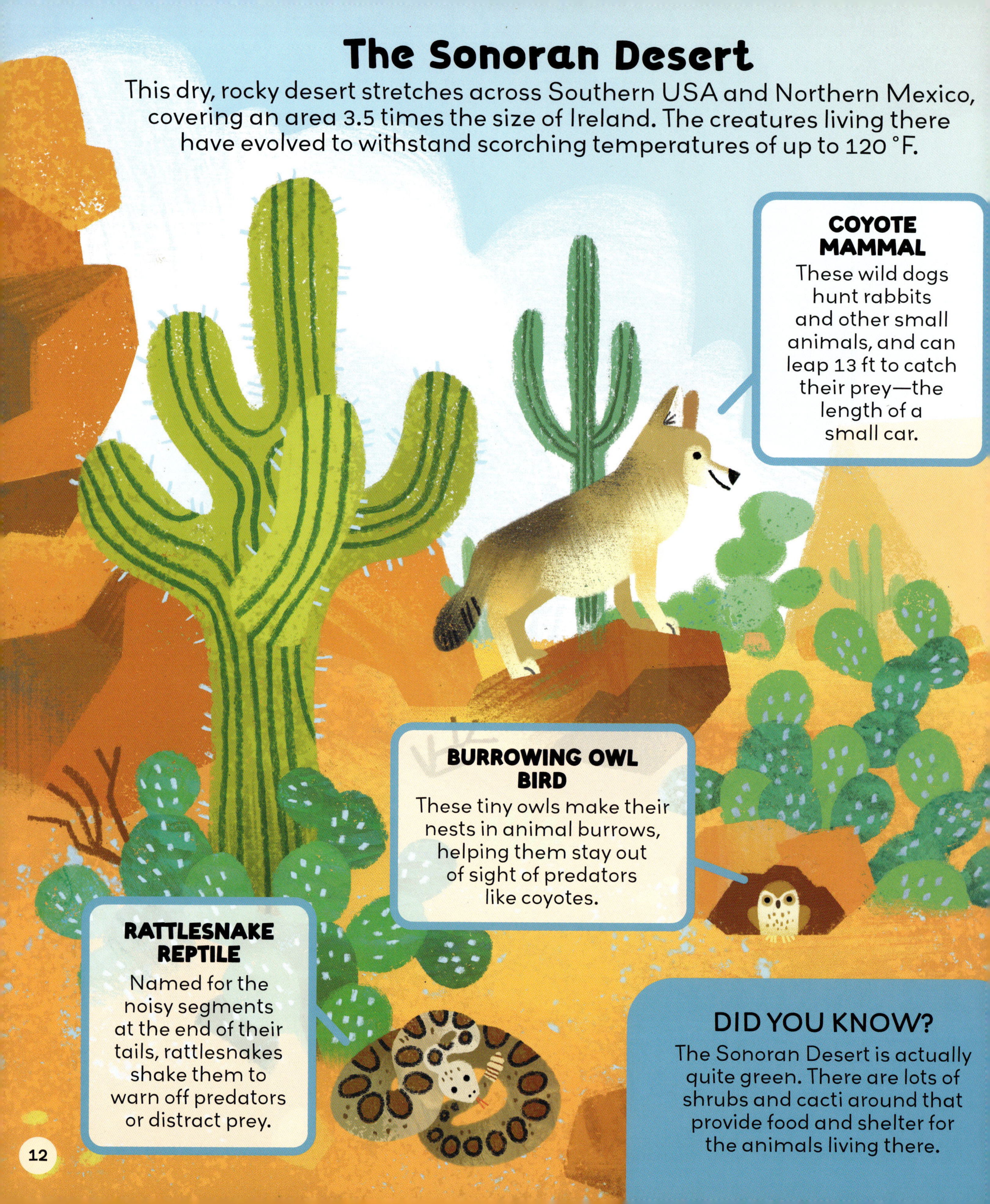

COYOTE
MAMMAL

These wild dogs hunt rabbits and other small animals, and can leap 13 ft to catch their prey—the length of a small car.

BURROWING OWL
BIRD

These tiny owls make their nests in animal burrows, helping them stay out of sight of predators like coyotes.

RATTLESNAKE
REPTILE

Named for the noisy segments at the end of their tails, rattlesnakes shake them to warn off predators or distract prey.

DID YOU KNOW?

The Sonoran Desert is actually quite green. There are lots of shrubs and cacti around that provide food and shelter for the animals living there.

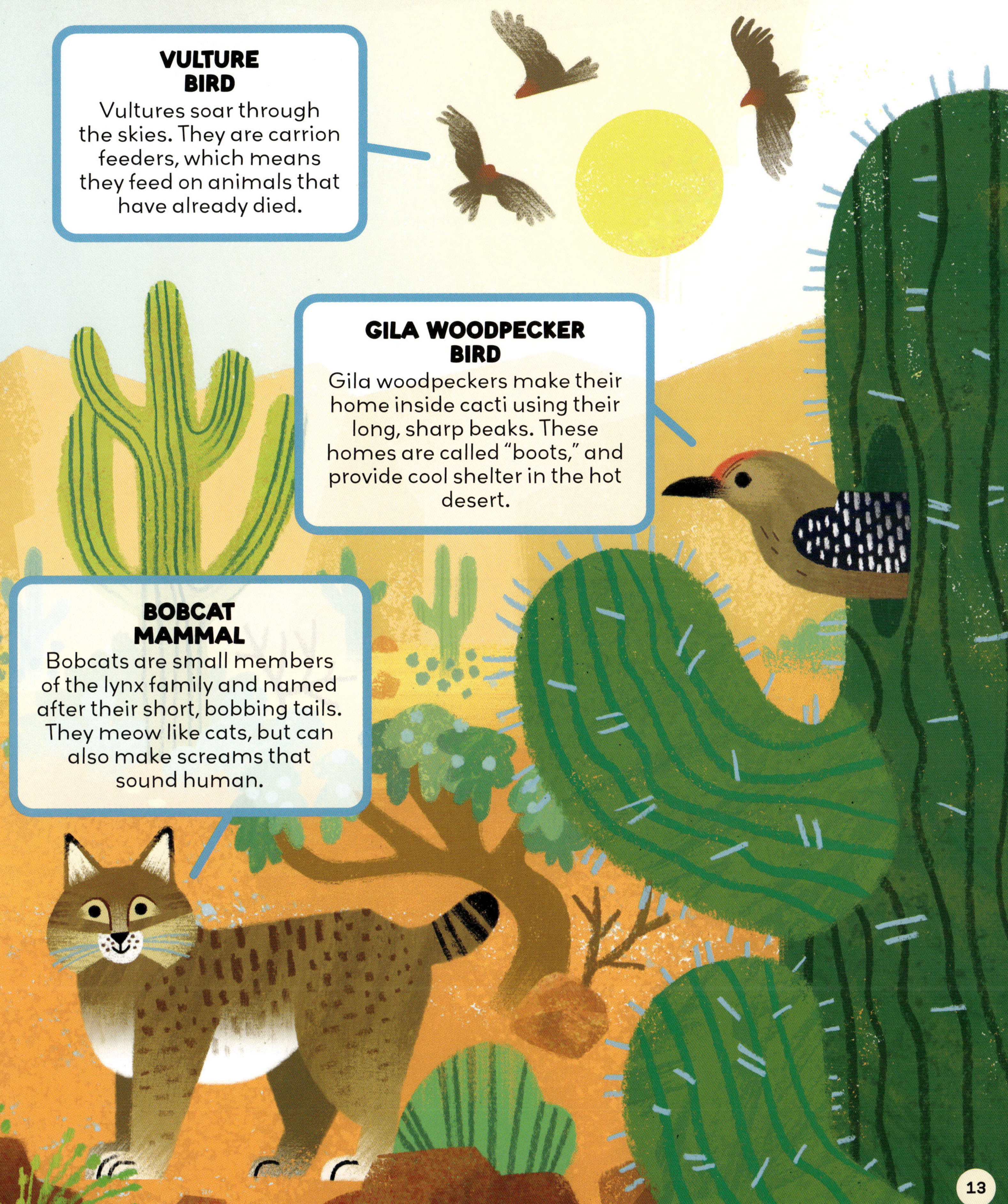
VULTURE
BIRD
Vultures soar through the skies. They are carrion feeders, which means they feed on animals that have already died.
GILA WOODPECKER
BIRD
Gila woodpeckers make their home inside cacti using their long, sharp beaks. These homes are called "boots," and provide cool shelter in the hot desert.
BOBCAT
MAMMAL
Bobcats are small members of the lynx family and named after their short, bobbing tails. They meow like cats, but can also make screams that sound human.

The Sahara Desert

This hot, sandy region covers around 3.6 million square miles of Africa, which is an area bigger than Australia. Animals get water from the food they eat, or by finding a rare oasis to drink from.

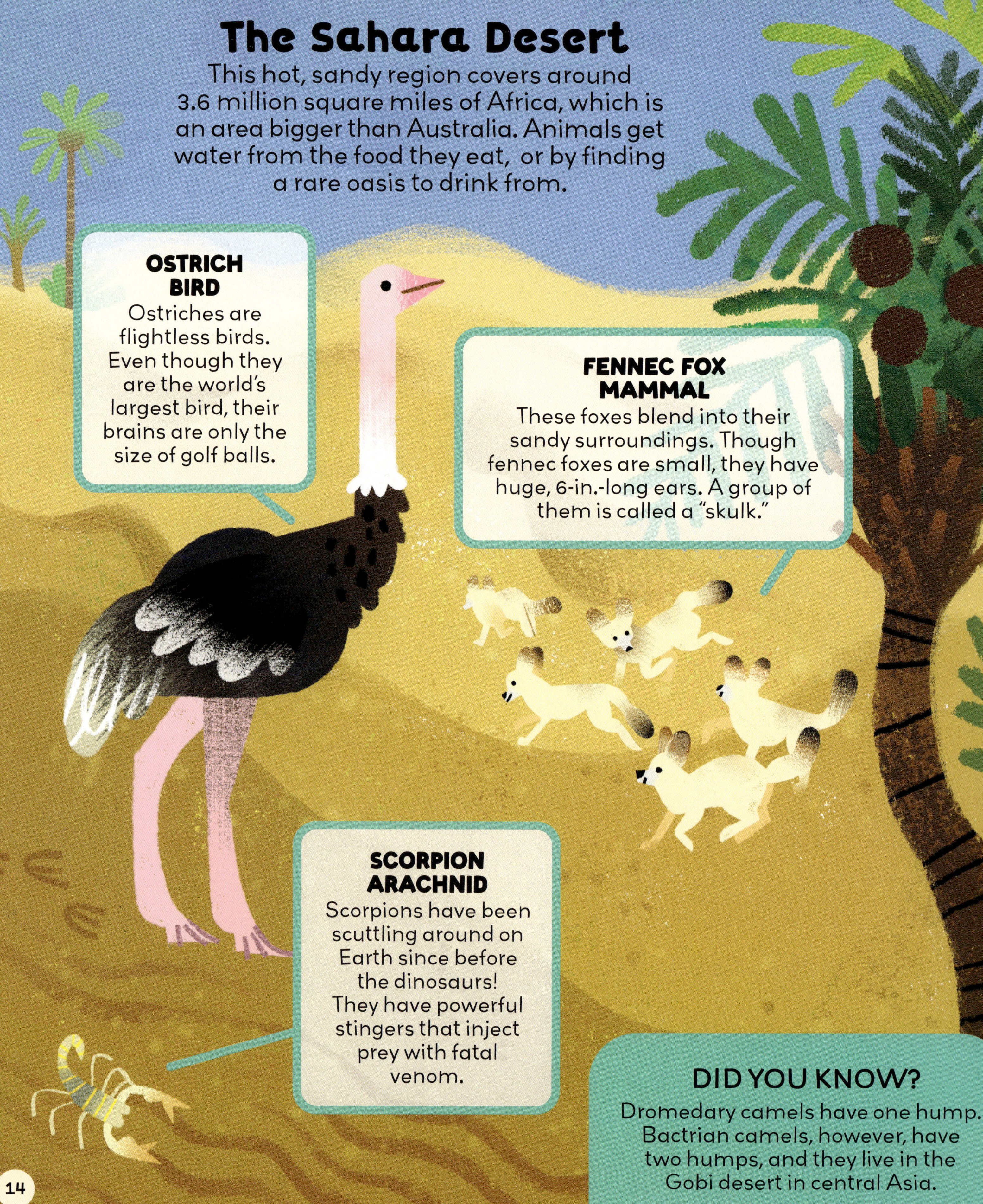

OSTRICH
BIRD

Ostriches are flightless birds. Even though they are the world's largest bird, their brains are only the size of golf balls.

FENNEC FOX
MAMMAL

These foxes blend into their sandy surroundings. Though fennec foxes are small, they have huge, 6-in.-long ears. A group of them is called a "skulk."

SCORPION
ARACHNID

Scorpions have been scuttling around on Earth since before the dinosaurs! They have powerful stingers that inject prey with fatal venom.

DID YOU KNOW?

Dromedary camels have one hump. Bactrian camels, however, have two humps, and they live in the Gobi desert in central Asia.

JERBOA
MAMMAL

These mouse-like rodents have long back legs to help them hop along the sand. They can leap 10 ft at a time!

ADDAX
MAMMAL

Also known as white or screwhorn antelopes, these desert dwellers boast striking horns up to 33 in. long.

SAHARAN STRIPED POLECAT
MAMMAL

This striped animal usually lives on the edges of the desert where the terrain is rockier. Like a skunk, it can spray a smelly liquid if it feels threatened.

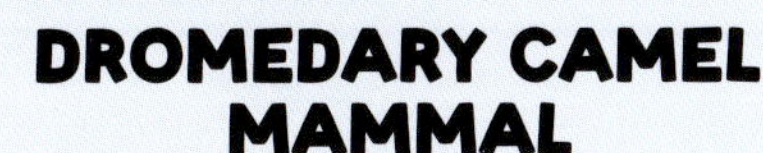

DROMEDARY CAMEL
MAMMAL

Camels are masters of survival. They have long eyelashes and can close off their nostrils to protect them from sandstorms. They can also store up to 80 lbs of fat in their humps, which they use as energy when food is scarce.

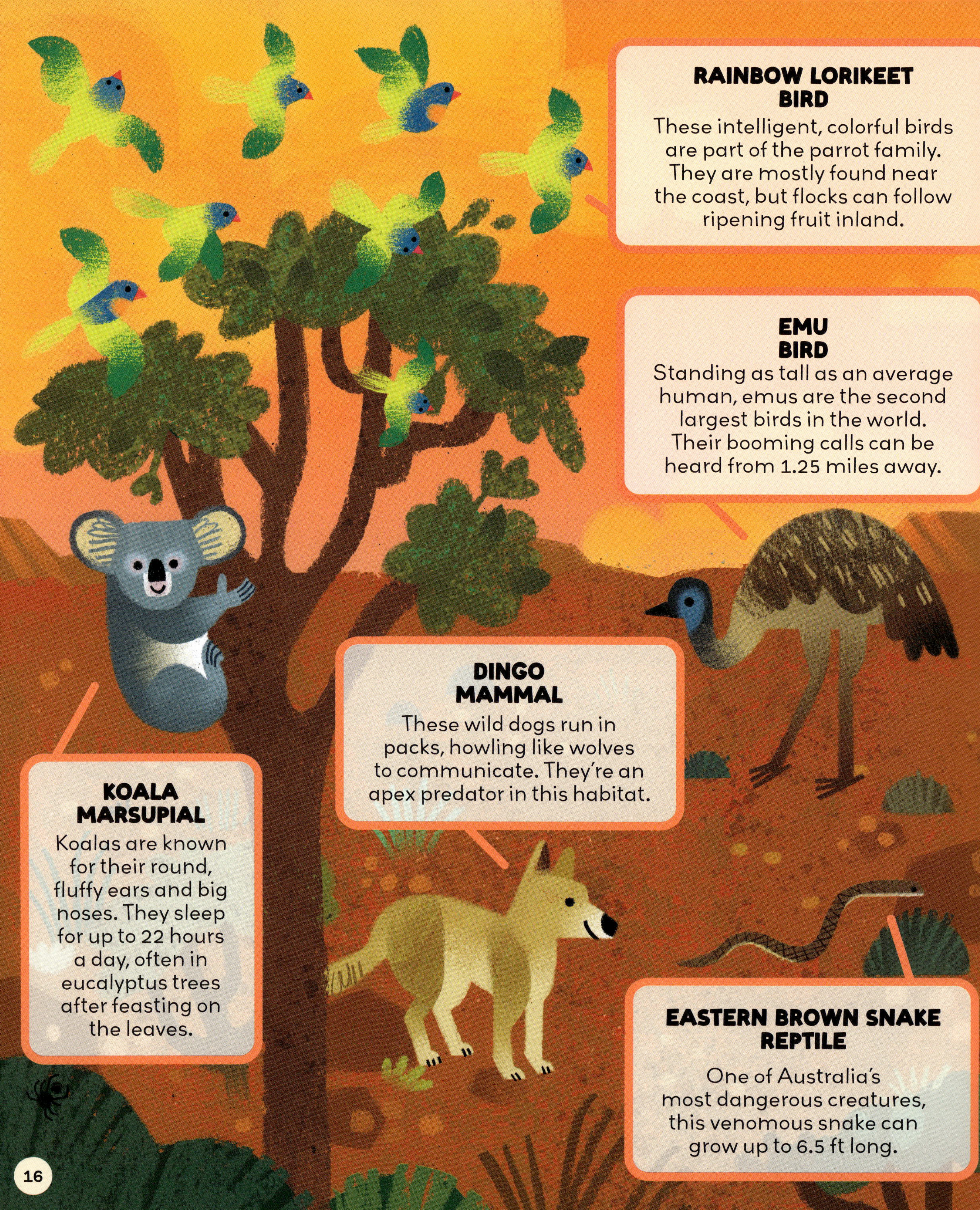
RAINBOW LORIKEET
BIRD
These intelligent, colorful birds are part of the parrot family. They are mostly found near the coast, but flocks can follow ripening fruit inland.
EMU
BIRD
Standing as tall as an average human, emus are the second largest birds in the world. Their booming calls can be heard from 1.25 miles away.
DINGO
MAMMAL
These wild dogs run in packs, howling like wolves to communicate. They're an apex predator in this habitat.
KOALA
MARSUPIAL
Koalas are known for their round, fluffy ears and big noses. They sleep for up to 22 hours a day, often in eucalyptus trees after feasting on the leaves.
EASTERN BROWN SNAKE
REPTILE
One of Australia's most dangerous creatures, this venomous snake can grow up to 6.5 ft long.

The Australian Outback

The Australian Outback is a rich blend of desert and grassland conditions. It covers around 2.16 million square miles, an area over 22 times the size of the UK. Temperatures in this vast territory range from 14 °F to 122 °F, so the animal species that live here have to adapt to all weathers.

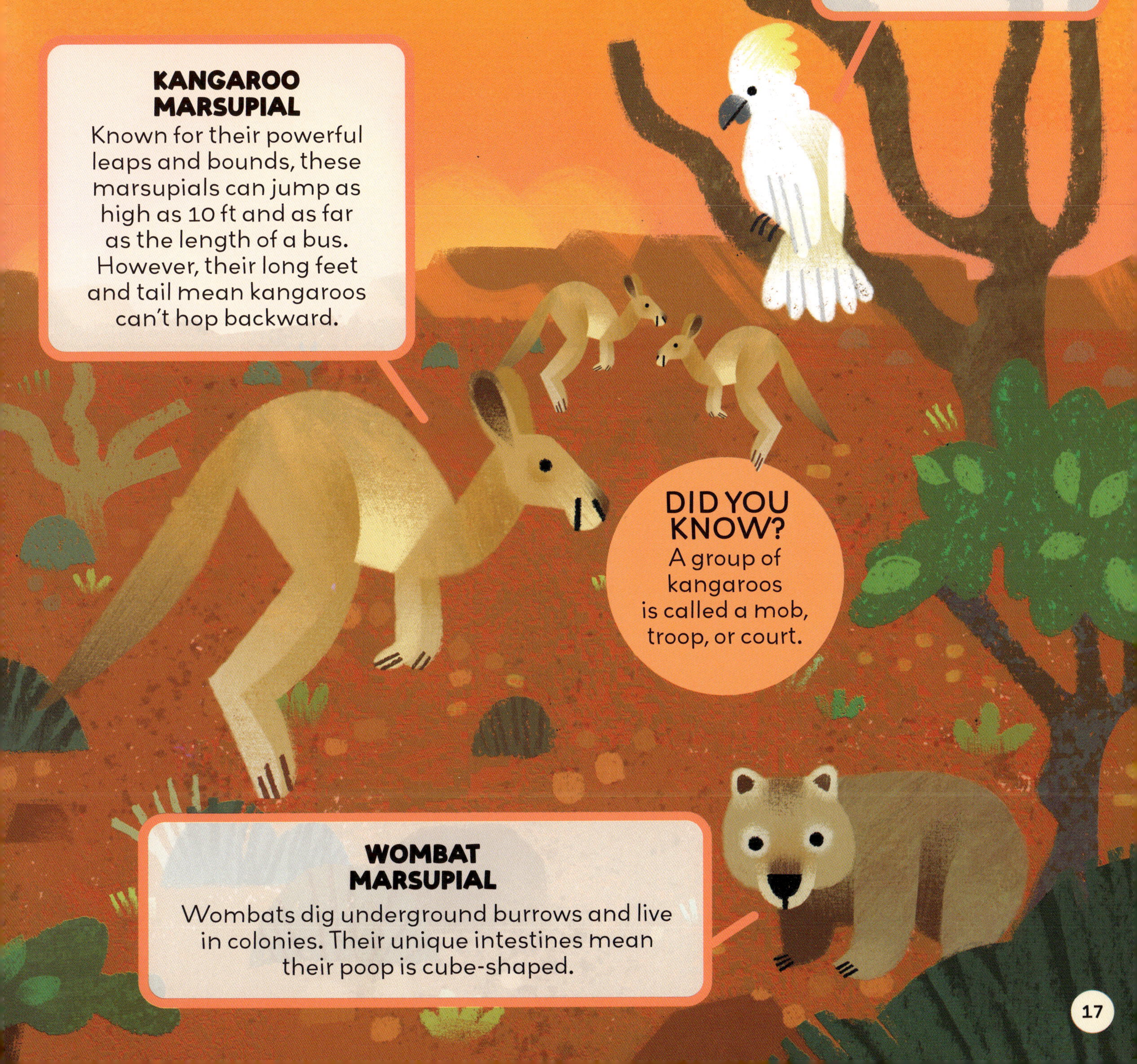

COCKATOO BIRD

These fancy parrots stand out due to the large yellow crests on their head. Cockatoos are very clever and can even be taught human words.

KANGAROO MARSUPIAL

Known for their powerful leaps and bounds, these marsupials can jump as high as 10 ft and as far as the length of a bus. However, their long feet and tail mean kangaroos can't hop backward.

DID YOU KNOW?

A group of kangaroos is called a mob, troop, or court.

WOMBAT MARSUPIAL

Wombats dig underground burrows and live in colonies. Their unique intestines mean their poop is cube-shaped.

Grassland Habitats

Savannahs are large areas of grassland located in or near tropical areas. They have some trees dotted around. Savannahs are found all over the world with the exception of Antarctica, and there are lots of different types . . .

TROPICAL SAVANNAHS

Africa's Serengeti region is a tropical savannah. These biomes are found close to the equator and do not receive a lot of rain. The animals who live there have to move around the area to find food and water.

TEMPERATE SAVANNAHS

Australia has areas of temperate savannah, also known as **prairies** or **steppe.** These regions are mostly grass with few trees, which provide food and shelter for the animals there.

DID YOU KNOW?

40 percent of Earth's landmass is grassland!

MEDITERRANEAN SAVANNAHS

Mediterranean savannahs like Portugal's Alentejo region are hot and dry in the summer, and mild and rainy in winter.

FLOODED SAVANNAHS

Flooded savannahs like the Pantanal region in South America are grasslands covered in water. They usually have lots of birds and amphibians.

MONTANE SAVANNAHS

Montane savannahs like the Eastern Anatolian montane steppe in Eurasia are high up in hilly regions, covered in shrubland. Animals have evolved to navigate rocky terrain.

HOOPOE BIRD

The hoopoe lives in the Alentejo savannah. It is known for its distinctive black, white, and orange feathers, and a long, unique bill that can dig in the soil to find bugs to eat.

BEZOAR IBEX MAMMAL

This wild goat lives in the Eurasian montane savannah region. Its huge 4 ft 7 in. horns are the animal kingdom's largest in relation to the animal's size.

RHINOCEROS MAMMAL

Rhinoceroses have huge horns on their heads that can grow as long as a baseball bat. They use their horns to defend themselves, as well as using them to dig for food and water.

ZEBRA MAMMAL

Zebras belong to the horse family. Each zebra has unique stripe markings that let other zebras know who they are, and help them hide in the long grass.

LION MAMMAL

Of all the big cats, lions are the only ones to live as families, or "prides." Lionesses rear their cubs together. Male lions are responsible for protecting the pride. The strongest fighters tend to have darker manes.

DID YOU KNOW?

Lions take advantage of noisy storms to sneak up on their prey.

The Serengeti

The hot, dry Serengeti region of Tanzania, Africa, is home to hundreds of animal species. Herds of zebras and gazelles follow the rains to find food—and meat-eaters, like lions and crocodiles, follow them. Serengeti animals drink and cool off at rivers and waterholes.

GIRAFFE
MAMMAL

Known for their long necks, giraffes can grow up to 18 ft tall—over three times as tall as the average human. This means they can reach the leaves at the top of the tallest trees.

ELEPHANT
MAMMAL

At up to 10 ft tall, African elephants are the world's heaviest land animal. You can easily tell them apart from their Asian cousins by their much bigger ears.

CROCODILE
REPTILE

Crocodiles lay eggs in the muddy banks of rivers and waterholes, and guard them until they hatch. They are apex predators in the Serengeti, lurking under the water to ambush unsuspecting drinkers.

The Pantanal

"Pantanal" comes from the Portuguese "pântano," meaning "wetlands" or "swamp." It's located in South America, covering around 54,000 square miles across Brazil, Bolivia, and Paraguay.

CROWNED SOLITARY EAGLE BIRD

Also known as the **Chaco eagle**, these endangered birds are known for their huge wingspans, which can stretch as wide as an average human is tall.

GIANT ANTEATER MAMMAL

Anteaters have strong front legs and claws to break open termite and ants' nests. They then use their 2-ft-long tongues to eat the insects inside.

Anteaters don't have teeth! They use their long, sticky tongues to eat instead.

CAPYBARA MAMMAL

At up to 174 lbs, capybaras are Earth's largest rodent. They can reach 4.25 ft long, and are usually found along riverbanks.

PIRANHA FISH

These fearsome fish vary in color from silvery to black, and can grow up to 2 ft long. Most piranhas scavenge their food rather than attacking animals, however!

HYACINTH MACAW BIRD

These bright blue birds are the largest flying parrots at 3 ft long. They eat seeds, fruit, and insects.

OCELOT MAMMAL

Standing a little larger than a pet cat, ocelots prowl the undergrowth at night, hunting for rodents and fish.

TAPIR MAMMAL

Tapirs are distantly related to horses and rhinos. Though shorter than their relatives, tapirs have bulky bodies and horse-like hooves.

GIANT RIVER OTTER MAMMAL

Giant otters are the largest members of the weasel family. They can grow up to 6 ft long! Their furry, webbed feet help propel them through the water.

Forest Levels

Woodlands and forests are generally divided into four layers. Most animals can move up and down through these layers, but spend most of their time in just one of them.

EMERGENT LAYER

This wet and windy layer is the highest part of a forest, where the tallest trees break through—or "emerge" from—the canopy. It doesn't provide much shelter, so it doesn't provide a suitable habitat for many animals or plants. However, you can find birds up here (along with some brave rainforest monkeys).

CANOPY LAYER

The canopy layer includes the branches and leaves of most trees, and can be around 100–150 ft high off the ground. Since it's quite sheltered from the weather, this layer is where most forest plants and animals live, like birds, reptiles, and some mammals like squirrels and lizards.

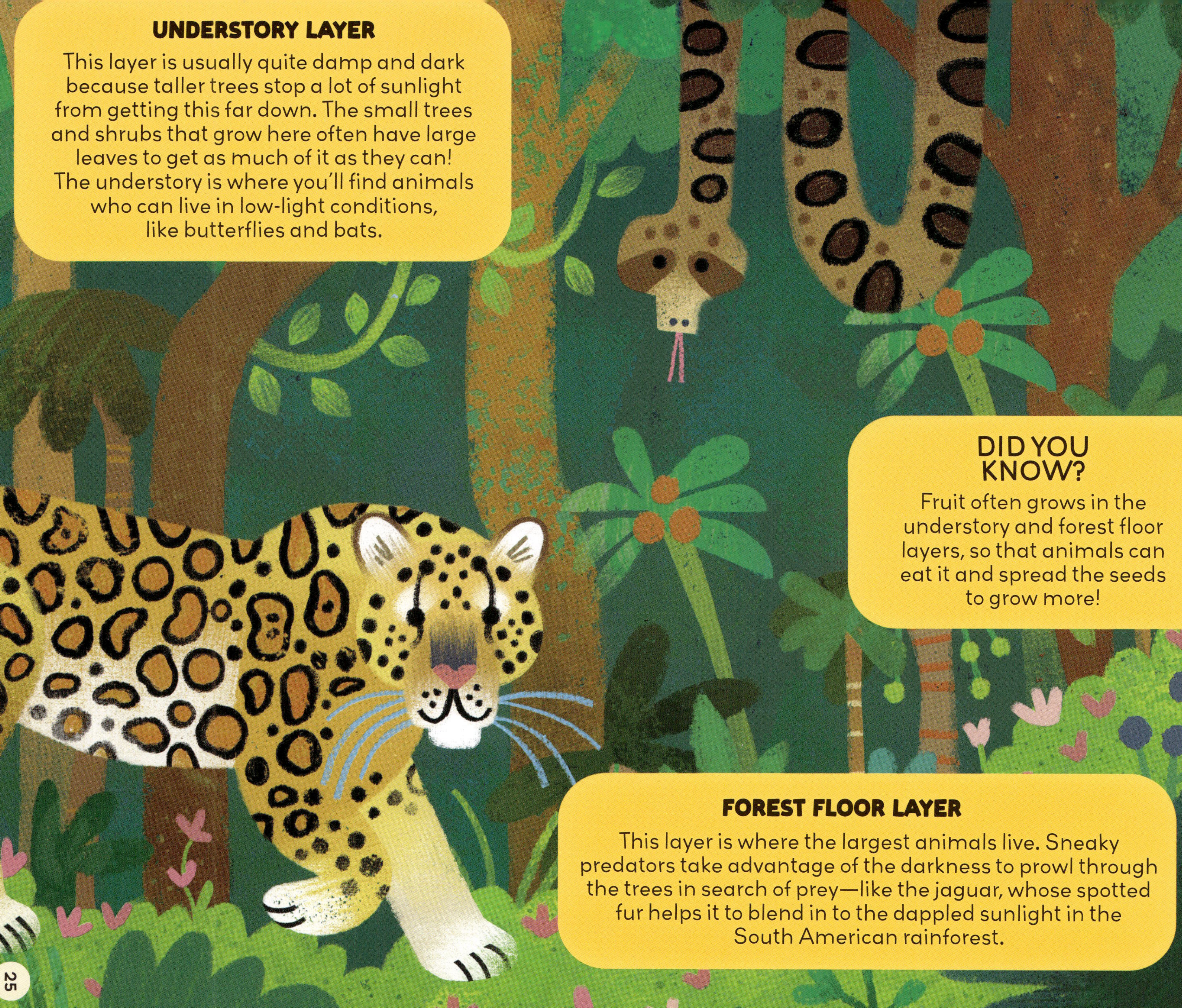

UNDERSTORY LAYER

This layer is usually quite damp and dark because taller trees stop a lot of sunlight from getting this far down. The small trees and shrubs that grow here often have large leaves to get as much of it as they can! The understory is where you'll find animals who can live in low-light conditions, like butterflies and bats.

DID YOU KNOW?

Fruit often grows in the understory and forest floor layers, so that animals can eat it and spread the seeds to grow more!

FOREST FLOOR LAYER

This layer is where the largest animals live. Sneaky predators take advantage of the darkness to prowl through the trees in search of prey—like the jaguar, whose spotted fur helps it to blend in to the dappled sunlight in the South American rainforest.

The Rainforests of Borneo and Sumatra

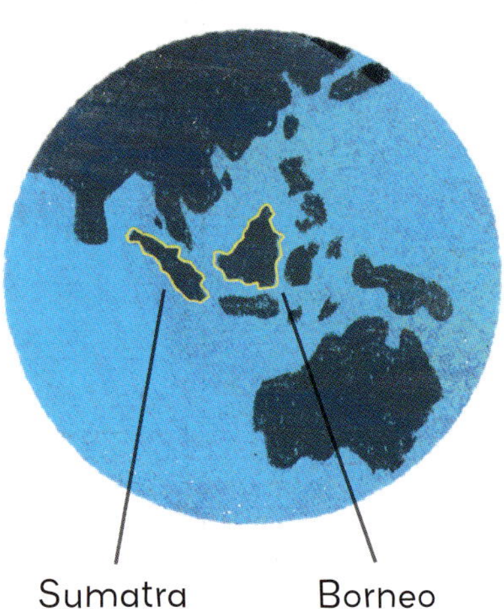

The rainforests of Southeast Asia are teeming with over 400 different animal species, including some of the world's oldest and rarest living things.

SUMATRA
Sumatra is the only wild place on Earth where tigers, rhinos, orangutans, and elephants live together.

SUMATRAN LEAF BIRD
BIRD

This colorful bird makes its home in the lowland forests of the island.

SUMATRAN RHINOCEROS
MAMMAL

Rare Sumatran rhinos have long hair, and are more closely related to the extinct woolly rhinoceros than any other rhinos around.

CLOUDED LEOPARD
MAMMAL

Clouded leopards are often found in the trees, slinking from branch to branch.

SUMATRAN TIGER
MAMMAL

Sumatran tigers are the smallest tigers, and also the rarest. It is thought there could be only 500 left in the wild.

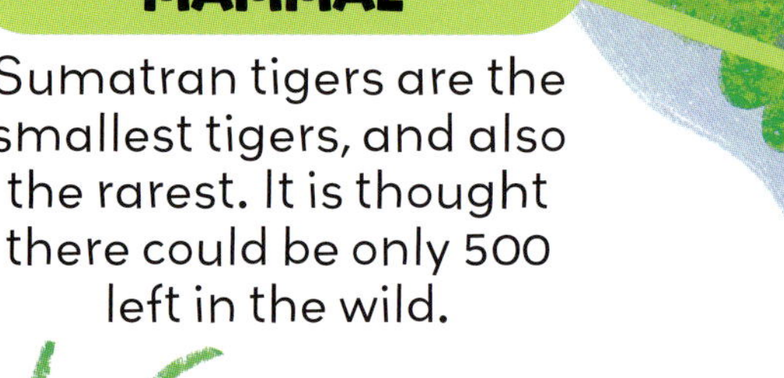

BORNEO

Borneo is the world's third largest island and is about as big as Turkey.

PROBOSCIS MONKEY MAMMAL

The male proboscis monkey's famously big nose can grow over 4 in. long and hangs down over their mouths. Female and baby proboscis monkeys have smaller, upturned noses.

FLYING FOX MAMMAL

Flying foxes don't use echolocation to find their food, instead they rely on their keen eyesight and sense of smell.

SUN BEAR MAMMAL

Sun bears have extra-long tongues to eat honey with.

ORANGUTAN MAMMAL

Orangutans weigh about as much as an average adult human. They build nests to sleep in at night.

DID YOU KNOW?

The **Bornean Red Carnivore** was spotted on camera in 2003, but no one has ever seen one since. Scientists think it's about the size of a cat, with dark red fur and a long bushy tail.

The Amazon Rainforest

The Amazon rainforest is the world's largest. It's so big that it spreads over nine South American countries, though most of the rainforest is in Brazil.

TOUCAN BIRD
This bright-beaked bird spends most of its life in the canopy layer. Its bill can be almost as long as its body!

HOWLER MONKEY MAMMAL
Howler monkeys have extra-loud calls to warn other monkeys to stay away. They can be heard from 3 miles away.

IGUANA REPTILE
These huge lizards can grow to be 6 ft 6 in. long, which means it could fill a queen-size bed from top to bottom.

BLUE MORPHO INSECT
These bright blue butterflies flutter through the understory, searching for rotting fruit to feed on.

ANACONDA REPTILE
Anacondas are the heaviest snakes in the world. They squeeze their prey by wrapping their long bodies around it very tightly.

DID YOU KNOW?

1 in 10 of all known animal species live in the Amazon rainforest, with more being discovered every year.

SLOTH
MAMMAL

Sloths are known for being some of the most relaxed animals around. They travel 0.2 miles a day—that's less than half of a soccer field.

BLUE POISON DART FROG
AMPHIBIAN

These tiny, poisonous frogs are deadly. Their brightly colored skin is a warning to other animals to stay away!

AGOUTI
MAMMAL

Agoutis are large rodents with hooflike claws. They live in burrows on the forest floor.

BLACK CAIMAN
REPTILE

Caimans are related to alligators and live in Central and South America. Black caimans are known for being the largest predators in the Amazon River.

Ocean Animals

Nearly 75 percent of the Earth's surface is water, with 97 percent of that water found in seas and oceans. This provides plenty of homes for some amazing animals . . .

MANATEE MAMMAL

Manatees have the same common ancestor as elephants. They drift through shallow water, sometimes so slowly that algae grows on them.

SEAHORSE FISH

Male seahorses carry the eggs. When the babies hatch, they hold each other's tails to stay together!

ARCTIC OCEAN

ATLANTIC OCEAN

PACIFIC OCEAN

STINGRAY FISH

These flat fish have sharp spines on their tails, which they use to defend themselves. Bigger rays can even pierce wooden boats!

SWORDFISH FISH

Swordfish are named for their long, flat bills, which they use to knock smaller fish out of their shoal to eat.

MAGNIFICENT FRIGATEBIRDS BIRDS

Known for their incredible red and black feathers, male magnificent frigatebirds make a drumming noise to attract a mate.

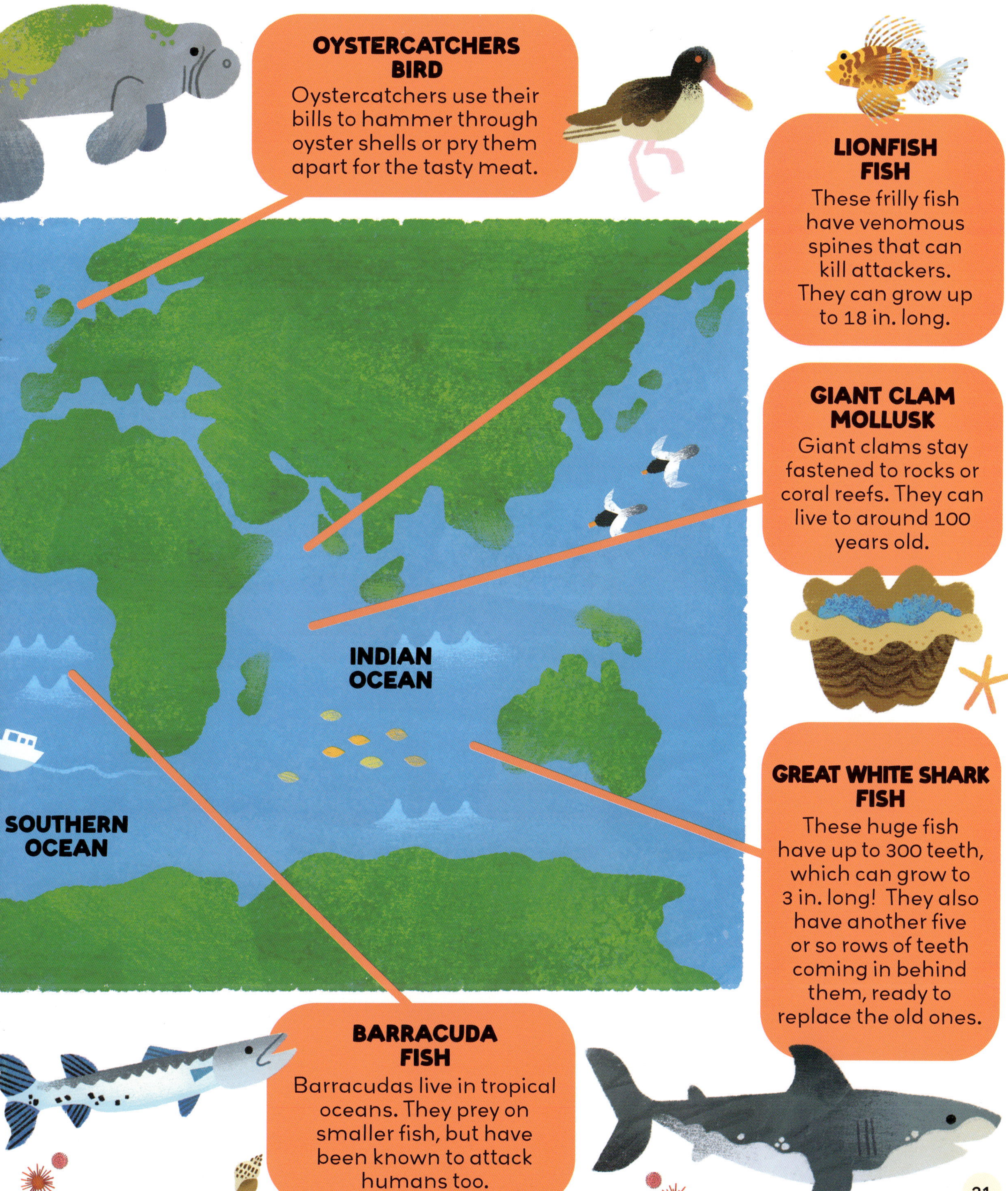
OYSTERCATCHERS
BIRD
Oystercatchers use their bills to hammer through oyster shells or pry them apart for the tasty meat.
LIONFISH
FISH
These frilly fish have venomous spines that can kill attackers. They can grow up to 18 in. long.
GIANT CLAM
MOLLUSK
Giant clams stay fastened to rocks or coral reefs. They can live to around 100 years old.
INDIAN
OCEAN
SOUTHERN
OCEAN
GREAT WHITE SHARK
FISH
These huge fish have up to 300 teeth, which can grow to 3 in. long! They also have another five or so rows of teeth coming in behind them, ready to replace the old ones.
BARRACUDA
FISH
Barracudas live in tropical oceans. They prey on smaller fish, but have been known to attack humans too.

Coral Reefs

Coral reefs are some of the most diverse places on Earth, with up to a quarter of ocean life making its home there. That's over a million species, including the coral itself, which is a living animal related to sea anemones.

REEF SHARK
FISH

These fearsome fish chase their prey into rocky holes to make it easier to grab them with their sharp teeth.

CLOWNFISH
FISH

The clownfish's bright colors warn attackers to stay away. They live in anemones, which can give predators a nasty sting.

BLUE TANG
FISH

Colorful blue tangs have special teeth that let them eat the harmful algae on corals. This makes them an important part of the coral reef because it helps keep the habitat healthy.

CROWN-OF-THORNS
STARFISH
ECHINODERM

Starfish are related to sea cucumbers. The crown-of-thorns is one of the biggest around. It feeds on coral, making it a dangerous resident of the reef.

BOX JELLYFISH
CNIDARIAN

Like coral, jellyfish are an invertebrate species related to anemones.

BOTTLENOSE DOLPHIN
MAMMAL

Dolphins have lungs, not gills, so they frequently have to come up to the surface to breathe.

COMMON OCTOPUS
MOLLUSK

Octopuses are very intelligent. Since they don't have bones, they can squeeze through holes as small as 1 in. across to escape predators.

ORNATE ROCK LOBSTER
CRUSTACEAN

Like humans, lobsters can be right- or left-handed (or both!). They have special receptors on their feet to help them find food.

STOUT INFANTFISH
FISH

These tiny fish are the world's smallest! They're as long as a pencil is wide.

Beneath the Waves

Did you know that humans have only explored **5 percent** of the ocean? There are so many creatures we have yet to meet, but here are some of the things that roam our seas . . .

WHALE SHARK
FISH

Whale sharks are the biggest fish around. They have huge mouths to feed on plankton.

BLUE WHALE
MAMMAL

Blue whales are the biggest animals on Earth! They can grow over 100 ft—or two semi-trucks—long.

SPERM WHALE
MAMMAL

Sperm whales sleep vertically in family groups called pods. This helps them stay camouflaged in dark, deep water.

GIANT SQUID
MOLLUSK
Giant squid can grow as big as a school bus! They live so far down that we very rarely see them.

JELLYFISH
CNIDARIAN
Jellyfish trail long, stinging tentacles behind them, which they use to share and paralyze their food.

BLOBFISH
FISH
Blobfish live around $^2/_3$ mile below the surface. They're thought of as the ugliest creature on Earth, but they only look like this out of water!

VAMPIRE SQUID
MOLLUSK
Vampire squid get their name from the cloak-like webbing around their arms.

ANGLERFISH
FISH
Female anglerfish have a glowing bulb that hangs over their huge mouths to attract prey in the pitch-black ocean.

Male anglerfish are tiny compared to the females!

DID YOU KNOW?
At around 7 miles deep, the Mariana Trench is the deepest point of the ocean. Mount Everest could fit in it!

River Animals

Rivers are essential habitats, not only for aquatic animals like amphibians and fish, but also as a food source for other creatures. Rivers offer plenty of places to live, from riverbanks and riverbeds, to trickling streams and estuaries. River water flows rather than sitting still (like a lake or pond), so the habitat moves and changes all the time.

HERON BIRD

You'll often find herons standing perfectly still among the reeds. They wait for fish to swim nearby, then quickly pluck them from the water with their long bills.

SALMON FISH

Salmon are some of the only fish that can survive in the waters of both rivers and oceans. They can jump out of the water to climb waterfalls.

MANATEE MAMMAL

Remember manatees from the ocean? They can actually swim between ocean and river water, so it's not unusual to find them a little further inland.

BEAVER
MAMMAL

Beavers' strong teeth help them chew down trees to build dams and lodges to live in.

FROG
AMPHIBIAN

Frogs have long, powerful legs that help them leap great distances. The South African sharp-nosed frog can jump up to 90 times its body length!

DUCK-BILLED PLATYPUS
MAMMAL

The platypus breaks the mammal mold—instead of live young, it lays eggs. Combined with its unique bill and large, flat tail, this led the first scientists who studied it to think it was a hoax!

The Ganges River

Flowing through India and Bangladesh, the Ganges is home to lots of weird and wonderful animals.

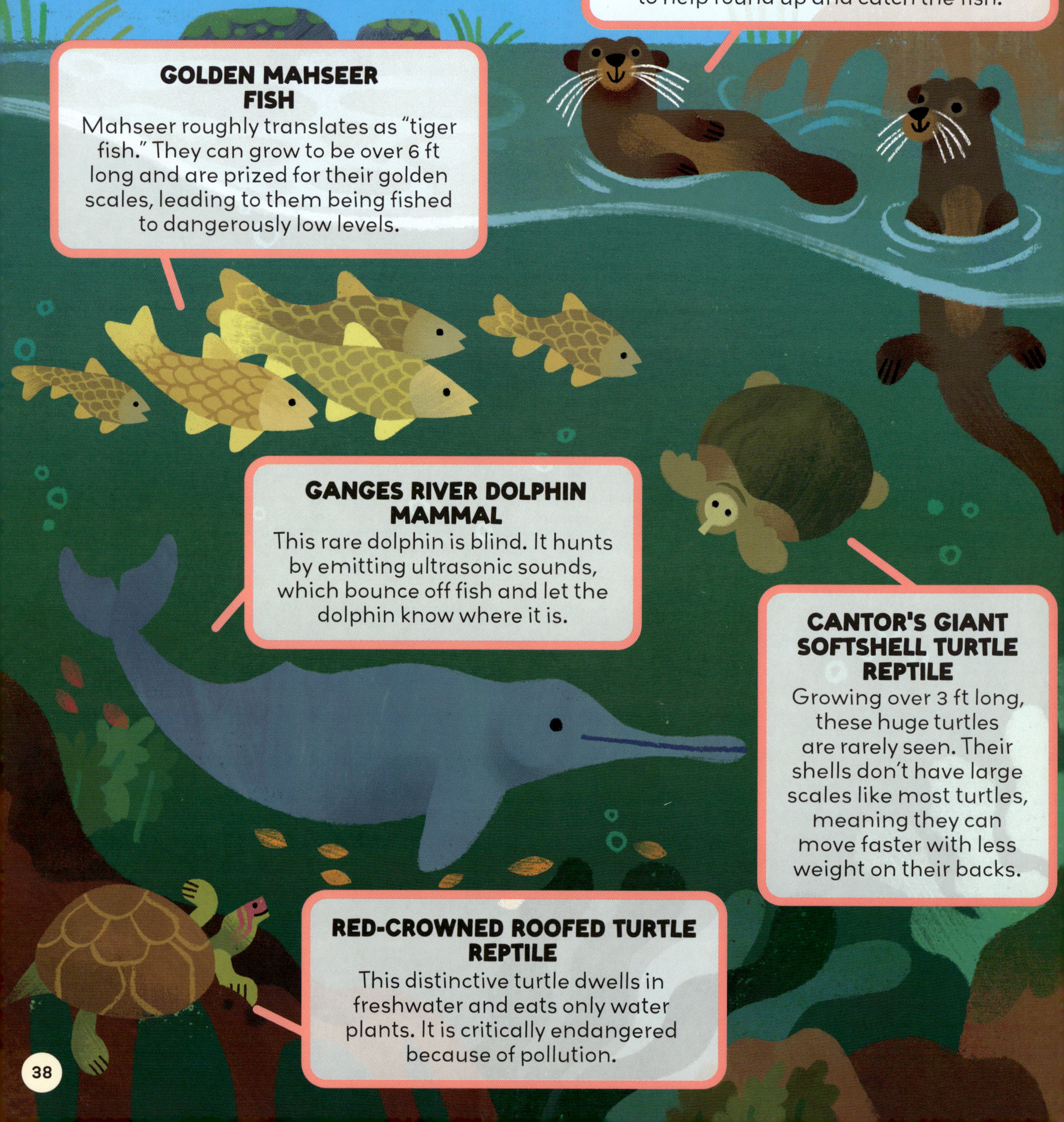

SMOOTH-COATED OTTER
MAMMAL

Smooth-coated otters are expert fishers. Groups of them swim in a V-formation to help round up and catch the fish.

GOLDEN MAHSEER
FISH

Mahseer roughly translates as "tiger fish." They can grow to be over 6 ft long and are prized for their golden scales, leading to them being fished to dangerously low levels.

GANGES RIVER DOLPHIN
MAMMAL

This rare dolphin is blind. It hunts by emitting ultrasonic sounds, which bounce off fish and let the dolphin know where it is.

CANTOR'S GIANT SOFTSHELL TURTLE
REPTILE

Growing over 3 ft long, these huge turtles are rarely seen. Their shells don't have large scales like most turtles, meaning they can move faster with less weight on their backs.

RED-CROWNED ROOFED TURTLE
REPTILE

This distinctive turtle dwells in freshwater and eats only water plants. It is critically endangered because of pollution.

The Nile River

The River Nile has been recognized as the longest river in the world—it is found in northeast Africa.

ROCK HYRAX
MAMMAL

These riverbank dwellers have dark scent glands on their back, which they rub on trees and rocks to mark their territory.

AFRICAN SACRED IBIS
BIRD

Sacred ibis were important to the ancient Egyptians, whose god of wisdom and the moon, Thoth, was shown with the head of an ibis.

NILE MONITOR
REPTILE

Nile monitors are large lizards, standing only a little smaller than Komodo dragons. They are strong swimmers and runners, which helps them catch prey like frogs and fish.

DID YOU KNOW?

Northeast Africa's famous river is the longest in the world, stretching for over 4,100 miles.

HIPPOPOTAMUS
MAMMAL

With a name meaning "river horse," these bulky mammals are the most dangerous land animal in the world due to their size and aggressiveness.

SADDLE-BILLED STORK
BIRD

These tall birds stand up to 6 ft 6 in. tall. They nest in trees and swoop down to hunt prey in the riverbed.

NILE CROCODILE
REPTILE

These crocodiles are the largest in Africa. They can reach 19 ft long and weigh as much as a cow.

The Himalayan Mountains

Central Asia's vast mountain range has some of the highest peaks in the world. The harsh environment means animals have to be tough to get by.

HIMALAYAN TAHR
MAMMAL

Tahrs look like big goats. They roam the mountains looking for plants to eat. In the winter, they stay near the bottom of the mountains where it's warmer and there's more food to be found.

GRIFFON VULTURE
BIRD

Griffon vultures glide high above the mountains. Their bendy necks help them gulp down rodents and other prey.

SNOW LEOPARD
MAMMAL

Snow leopards have pale, spotted fur that helps them blend into the mountainside. Their huge feet stop them from sinking into the snow.

YAK
MAMMAL

Yaks are covered in thick, shaggy hair that helps keep them warm at high altitudes. They roam higher than any other mammal.

HIMALAYAN MONAL
BIRD

These colorful birds are also known as **danphes**. Male monals use their bright tail feathers as part of a dance to attract a mate.

PIKA
MAMMAL

Tiny pikas are related to rabbits, though they don't have the same powerful back legs. They're about the same size as a guinea pig.

The Andes Mountains

The Andes mountain range in South America is the longest in the world, providing homes for thousands of animal species.

ANDEAN COCK-OF-THE-ROCK
BIRD

These bright birds have large orange crests on their heads. Their strong claws help them grip onto trees and rocks.

ANDEAN CONDOR
BIRD

Andean condors are among the world's biggest flying birds, with a huge wingspan of up to 10 ft. This helps them glide for over 100 miles without needing to flap!

SPECTACLED BEAR
MAMMAL

Spectacled bears are named for the white rings around their eyes. They're the only bears native to South America.

HUEMUL
MAMMAL

These short deer are very rare. They group together on the mountain plains for safety from predators like cougars.

LLAMAS VS ALPACAS
MAMMAL

Both llamas and alpacas are related to camels. They're known for their fuzzy features and wool. Alpacas are smaller than llamas and have shorter ears. Llamas are stronger and can carry heavy loads for human farmers.

FLAMINGO
BIRD

Flamingos start with white or gray feathers. Over the years, they turn rosy pink from the food they eat.

CHINCHILLA
MAMMAL

Chinchillas are rodents known for their very thick, very fluffy fur. It keeps them warm in their chilly habitat.

The Arctic

Located at the top of the planet, the Arctic region is home to a wide range of creatures who have had to adapt to temperatures below −94 °F.

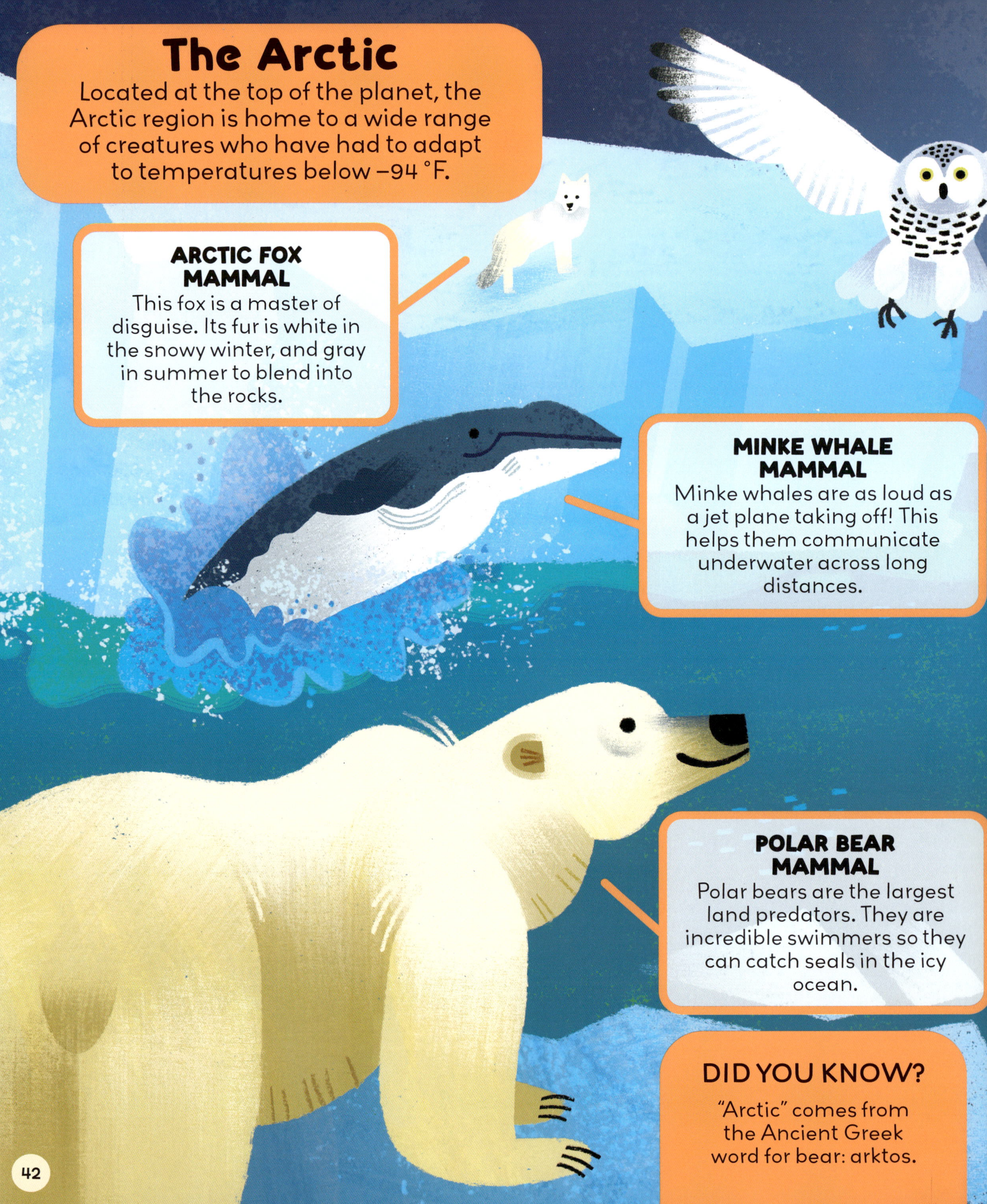

ARCTIC FOX
MAMMAL

This fox is a master of disguise. Its fur is white in the snowy winter, and gray in summer to blend into the rocks.

MINKE WHALE
MAMMAL

Minke whales are as loud as a jet plane taking off! This helps them communicate underwater across long distances.

POLAR BEAR
MAMMAL

Polar bears are the largest land predators. They are incredible swimmers so they can catch seals in the icy ocean.

DID YOU KNOW?

"Arctic" comes from the Ancient Greek word for bear: arktos.

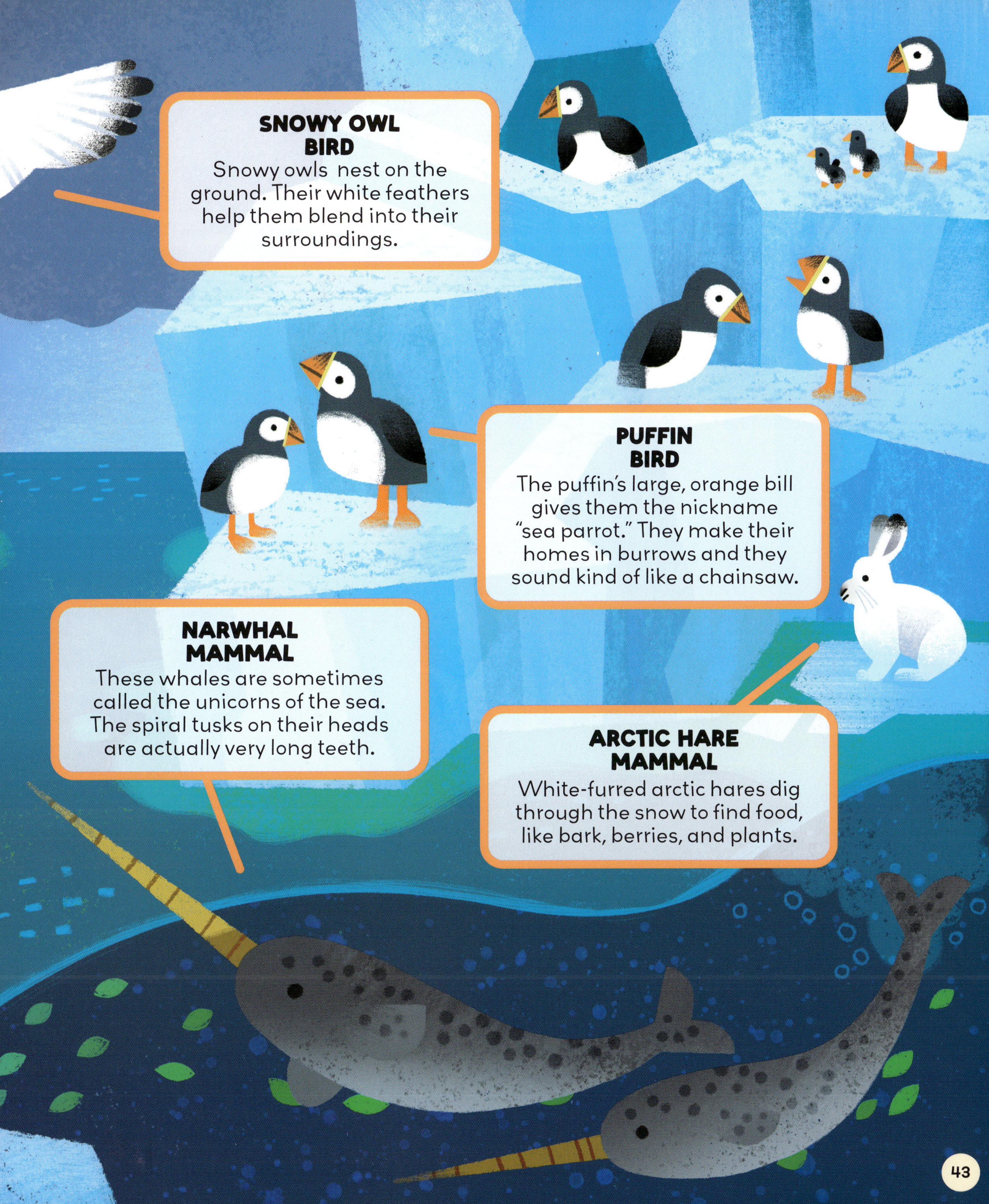
SNOWY OWL
BIRD
Snowy owls nest on the ground. Their white feathers help them blend into their surroundings.
PUFFIN
BIRD
The puffin's large, orange bill gives them the nickname "sea parrot." They make their homes in burrows and they sound kind of like a chainsaw.
NARWHAL
MAMMAL
These whales are sometimes called the unicorns of the sea. The spiral tusks on their heads are actually very long teeth.
ARCTIC HARE
MAMMAL
White-furred arctic hares dig through the snow to find food, like bark, berries, and plants.

The Antarctic

Antarctica is the driest, coldest, and windiest continent on Earth. It's also the largest desert, with only around a month's worth of rain per year. This makes for a harsh environment for its animals!

EMPEROR PENGUIN
BIRD
Male emperor penguins take care of the eggs while the females hunt for food. They tuck it into their skin at their feet to keep it warm for around two months.

GENTOO PENGUIN
BIRD
Gentoo penguins use pebbles to "propose" to their mates. If the female says yes, the pair will include the pebble in their rocky nests.

DID YOU KNOW?
Over 99 percent of the land in Antarctica is covered in snow and ice.
ROCKHOPPER PENGUIN
BIRD
These penguins are named for their tendency to hop around their rocky habitats. They can jump around 6 ft in a single bound!
ORCA
MAMMAL
Despite also being known as "killer whales," orcas are actually members of the dolphin family. They have been known to team up to hunt seals and penguins.
LEOPARD SEAL
MAMMAL
Dangerous leopard seals are some of the largest on the planet, with some females weighing more than a black bear! They make hooting noises to find a mate.

Index